Sahith Read it Wrong

Written By
Jo Oliver-Yeager, MS

Other Books By Jo Oliver-Yeager

Sophie Counts Her Steps
Adam (Sometimes) Can't Sit Still
Devon Missed the Joke

Copyright © 2021 Kind Words Publishing
ISBN 978-1-7358815-7-7

All rights reserved. This book may not be reproduced in whole or in part in any form, or by any means, without express written permission from the publisher.

Published by:

Kind Words Publishing
kindwordspublishing@gmail.com

This is dedicated to all the wonderful people with Dyslexia.

This book is one in a series intended to educate people about acceptance and understanding as well as giving a voice to anyone who may not fit into that "neat little box."

Embrace differences.

For my wonderful Tony and the inspiration of my three babies who hold my heart- Nyan, Tessa, & Auden for always supporting my love of writing.

Sahith wasn't a great reader. He didn't like to read.

It was especially bad when the teacher asked him to read in class. He acted like he didn't care, but he did care.

He wanted to be able to read, but things were harder for him than for his friends or classmates.

One day, as the class was going over their answers from the latest homework, the teacher called on Sahith. He was already worried he would be called on.

He knew what was going to happen. He would attempt to read the question and hope he knew the answer. Sahith had not done the homework.

In fact, there were many times he would be unable to do it.

The next day, Sahith's parents pulled him aside to talk about a letter that they received from his teacher.

The teacher shared copies of some of his written work. Her letter described some concerns she had about what could be going on with Sahith.

Sahith didn't understand what was going on.

Was he in trouble? There was concern that he may have some differences that were affecting his ability to read.

Sahith worried he was sick.

His parents took him to the eye doctor to make sure his vision was good. It was.

His parents took him to his pediatrician to make sure he was healthy. He was.

They decided to reach out to the school and ask for help.

Sahith's school scheduled a visit with the school psychologist.

"Maybe I am just stupid," he thought to himself.

Sahith and his parents had a visit to meet the school psychologist for the first time. She scheduled testing for Sahith the next day.

"Do you think something is wrong with me?" He asked her.

The school psychologist smiled and said, "No, I don't. I think you may do things differently, but that is not bad or wrong."

This reassured Sahith a bit more. He was still worried there was something wrong with him.

She gave Sahith several tests to check his reading and his writing.

He struggled to do them, but he knew he wanted answers to why his friends could read and write easily.

The next day, Sahith's parents pulled him aside. They had heard from the school. They had some answers that would make things clearer for Sahith.

He had something called Dyslexia.

It caused Sahith to see letters and numbers differently. It made it harder for him to process words to be able to read and write.

The good news, though, was there were many ways to support Sahith.

One way that Sahith's school was going to help him was with a reading specialist.

He would meet with one during school to help him learn how to read a different way.

He would use a laptop in class to help with his problems with writing.

After a few weeks, Sahith was starting to see progress.

He was able to read out loud with his reading specialist more than before. He also realized he was not stupid.

Book reports would be due in a month. Sahith wanted to present his book to the class.

This motivated him to find new skills.

He continued working with the reading specialist.

Sahith had chosen *Stuart Little* for his book report. He practiced reading it out loud and worked on being able to write out what he thought of the book.

It took him a little bit longer, but he completed the book in time to work on the report. Now all he had to do was present his report to the class.

At first, Sahith worried he would have to memorize what to say in case he froze and couldn't read his report.

He practiced every night with his parents.

He drew a picture of Stuart in a canoe, like the cover of the book.

Art was not his strong point, but he managed to make a nice cover for his book report.

As the day approached for his book report presentation, Sahith was ready.

He had practiced a few times before his class with his reading specialist to be sure.

When his teacher called on him, Sahith stood up.

He grabbed his report and walked to the front of the class. He showed off the cover he drew and started to describe the book.

He opened the report and read what he had written. Although he was choppy in sections, he managed to finish the presentation.

His classmates raised their hands and cheered at the great book report.

Sahith felt proud of his hard work.

Reading and writing would be a struggle in his life. He might do it differently than other people, but that won't stop him.

He felt empowered to find other ways to do those tasks.

Resources

- International Dyslexia Association
  https://dyslexiaida.org/

- The Dyslexia Foundation
  https://dyslexiafoundation.org/

- Learning Disabilities Association of America (LDA)
  https://ldaamerica.org/disabilities/dyslexia/

- The Lucy Project
  https://www.lucyproject.org/

- Dyslexia Advocation
  https://www.soallcanread.org/

- Dyslexic Advantage
  https://www.dyslexicadvantage.org/

www.ingramcontent.com/pod-product-compliance
Lightning Source LLC
Chambersburg PA
CBHW051300110526
44589CB00025B/2891